**Peace is the result of retraining your mind to process life as it is, rather than as you think it should be.**

Dr. Wayne W. Dyer

This book if dedicated to the victims and families of the Covid-19 virus.

It is also dedicated to the Calvary of first responders and essential personnel who have selflessly risen above expectations any of us could have ever imagined or hoped for. Their dedication, devotion and spirit have given new meaning to the word "service". They are the personification of suffering and bravery walking side by side.

# Contents

# Preface

It Is May 2020; the world is in the thrust of a nightmare pandemic called Covid-19 that just a few short months ago the world could never have imagined.  Life as we know it, is rapidly disappearing and it seems evident we all need to create a new one. Isolation, quarantine and death have revealed with a harsh clarity what we have lost. Everyone is trying to recapture the things we lost while embracing the things we had often overlooked and took for granted. We are trapped in a "broken recording" of sameness. Same people, same room, same routines. Some of us have surrendered to this, others have embraced the reopening of our cities and towns, some of us reluctantly doing so at a distance of six feet, while others pretending that people are not really dying or that the virus is not real. Regardless, we are all looking through a kaleidoscope desperately searching for a glimpse of the life we once knew and sorely miss.

 As I write this, there are approximately 5,500,000 worldwide cases of this virus and over 346,000 worldwide deaths, of which approximately 1,700,000 cases and over 100,000 deaths are in the United States.  Isolation and Social Distancing are the newest and most popular words of the day.  This virus has reached every continent. Offices and factories have shut down. Hospitals are scrambling for equipment and beds. Millions of people have lost their jobs. Daily life has been upended. Governments around the world are reacting differently to this crisis. In the United States, the federal government has enacted a financial recovery plan designed to stimulate the economy, the likes of which has never been seen in history. The world is desperately struggling for a cure for this virus with no clear remedy in sight. Most of us are filled with fear, frustration and doubt as to where this virus will go and how long it will last. Life as we know it, not only has changed, but continues to be redefined on a daily basis. The world's economies are at best sputtering along; people of all nations are suffering not only economically, but physically, emotionally and spiritually as well. People pray that their children, their families and their loved ones will not be the next victims of this virus. Socialization has traded places with loneliness. Trust has been replaced with fear, and understanding has been replaced with doubt. Life as we knew it has changed.

Our world leaders oftentimes are in disagreement with our scientists, our researchers and our medical professionals as to what to do. A course of action is at best a hunch or guided by issues such as politics and economics as opposed to health. People of all nations are confused as to where they stand or who to believe. Confusion, fear and no clear direction is taking root. Society has a new appreciation to those people and professions who have selflessly dedicated their own lives so that we can survive.

These people have gone beyond routine care and doing their jobs. They have instead fulfilled a self- imposed achievement beyond anyone's expectations. Here in the United States, our president has given each of our fifty governors the power to decide what to do. These governors in turn have relinquished control over public openings of our businesses and economies to the counties and towns in their state, further compounding a unified and coherent plan to combat this virus. The opening of our economies has been fraught with tensions between urban and rural areas and unease among businesses and the public. Many workers are left grappling with the impossible choice between their health and their livelihood.

There appears to be no order, only confusion. We live in a democratic society that insures personal freedoms and civil liberties to all. These freedoms and liberties are being greatly tested right now, without any clear cut solution that will not infringe on someone or something. Do we preserve our individual civil liberties at the expense of society? Do we preserve our economy or do we protect our health? These are the questions of the day. And instead of being united by grief, we have become divided by doubt and uncertainty. It seems our world is stuck in a fog that we cannot see our way out of. The destruction and disorder this pandemic has created will continue to change us in ways we cannot yet fully imagine. It is my personal view at this moment in time, that the full extent of this confusion has not even begun, as different governors decisions will not only conflict with each other, but will be challenged by people and families from their state who differ from their viewpoints. The world is frantically seeking a miracle that will free us from this nightmare and return our civilization to normalcy.

I have oftentimes thought about how I could help our society in this turbulent time. Help in a way beyond just mere isolation and social distancing. How can I make a difference? As I pondered this question over and over, the answer, although different and not what I had envisioned, became very clear to me. My decision has been guided by the proverb…" To the world you are only one person, but to one person, you could be the world". I felt that in this environment of confusion and self- doubt, if I could create a mechanism to give people even a glimmer of hope, not only during this crisis, but for years to come, by visions and life experiences of people whose eyesight has been replaced with insight, then I could accomplish my goal. It is in answer to this question that I put pen to paper and begin this book.

The chapters in this book are not written by me. They are written by trusted friends whose opinions I cherish and respect. My intent was not to give my friends an assignment, but to tap into their visions and life lessons as to what one thing they each felt is really important in life, that if by sharing it, could make a positive difference in at least one other life, especially during this pandemic. As my mind delved further into this question, I saw countless additional benefits that not only would be shared during this crisis, but for people to learn and value for years to come. I have experienced first- hand in life the effect that another person's care and concern can have, especially in difficult times where the kindest and simplest words can make all the difference.

The chapters contained herein reflect the words and insights of the authors. They have been written with the intent to make a difference. The authors are not celebrities or famous in any way. Their names would not be recognized by the general population. Each one of them possesses a wealth of knowledge that has nothing to do with dollars, but comes from perspective. In these dark times, that we're all traveling through together, these authors are truly a beacon of light. They each know that the ripple effect their stories provide, really matters. They are ordinary people who possess extraordinary visions.

When I was pondering whether to write this book, my mind was filled with doubt as to its merit. But once I had contacted the various authors and received their overwhelming support and enthusiasm, I became empowered that this endeavor was as right as I originally thought it was. I was delighted to find that not only did the authors exceed my expectations, but by allowing total control over everything and anything they wrote, and by writing with their minds and heart, their thoughts and their words became dimensionless, thereby creating the magic I had hoped to create.

It is our collective hope, that in some way, each one of these stories touches at least one of you, and provides you with the vision to positively impact your life.


Tom Fallarino

# Go Where You Are Celebrated, Not Tolerated

As we all share in the experience of isolation during this Pandemic, we also share in the contemplation that each of us has had time to enjoy. I use the word enjoy in hopes that most people choose to dwell upon the positive while we are surrounded by all the negative, serious, and frightening news we receive daily. This time of quiet, self-assessment should help us manage all the bumps in the road that we will experience in our lifetimes.

Life is a journey, and as many have described – a roller coaster. None of us will go through life without experiencing the highs and lows, the joys and sorrows, the richer and poorer times. It's how we manage each of those stages that make a difference in the journey we create for ourselves. If I were to give advice, it would be to "stay true to yourself and your convictions, and to keep yourself in the company of positive strong people." My motto has always been "Go where you are celebrated, not where you are tolerated." The support you will receive from those who love you is strength to overcome anything.

I've learned much about myself through other people. When asked for feedback in others' assessment of me, I received the word "tenacity" more often than any other. Actually, that is what got me through my challenges of life. I've been poor, wealthy, sick, healthy, alone, abused, frightened, excited; and through each period was focused on what was important to me, my sons. I was going to get through anything life threw at me, but nothing would stop me from giving them the best life I could.

Never accept the word "No". As Cher said; "No is just some bullshit word that somebody made up." I was told I couldn't attend college, for financial reasons. So I decided to work, and went to school at the same time. After each degree, I continued until I achieved my MBA and two other professional certificates. At work, I was told I would never be promoted in an "old boy school" type of work environment. So, I took on more responsibility than anyone else, became the go-to person, and was eventually promoted to the highest level in my department.

Perseverance. Stay true to your heart's desire. Look for support and help from those around you, and keep looking until you find what makes you happy. Luke 11:5; "If you keep knocking long enough, you will receive what you need because of your shameful perseverance". You know where you want to go and if you don't it's probably because you aren't listening. There is too much noise in our daily lives, too much competition; too much busy-ness. Take time out to listen, it's amazing what you will hear.

Bill Gates failed at his first business. Jim Carrey was at one time homeless. Oprah Winfrey was molested as a child, a pregnant teenager at age 14, then lost her child. Bethany Hamilton had her arm bitten off by a shark, then won first place in a surfing competition. Steven King's first novel was rejected 30 times. Trauma, abuse, poverty can all be turned into triumphs.

Pay it forward. If we all did good deeds, helped others who are less fortunate than ourselves, and treated others as we want to be treated, this world would be a better place. One last quote, from the movie Bohemian Rhapsody; "..Good thoughts, good words, good deeds..".

Ginny Bartoldus

# I Was Told... I Am Linda

When I was born, I was told I was Linda. Then I was told I was this and that. And I believed it and worked hard to be it. But that is not who I was born to be, not who I really am. Let me tell you a story, and then you will understand the importance of those six little words.

I was about eight years old. I had just taken a test in school and was so proud of my score and so proud of myself. My family was sitting at the kitchen table eating dinner and with pride I shared my accomplishment with them. My mother's response was, "well you think you are so smart, I know so much more than you do". Little Linda was devastated. And I remember those cutting words and I made a story out of them instead of just accepting it as a statement from my insecure mother. But then again, I was a child and kids believe their parents.

I went through most of my life believing this story...that I was less than. I felt "less than" in almost everything in my life. I wasn't smart enough, I wasn't pretty enough, I wasn't thin enough. And I was trying to prove to my mother, to myself, and then the entire world, that I was enough.

One day, after decades of believing and endless hours and many dollars working on myself, the lightbulb went off. I learned that just because my mother said it, didn't make it true. It was a projection of her reality, not mine. I made a decision and tossed out this story and my personal history of self-imposed deficiencies and realized my life was a series of steps I needed to take to bring me to the present realization of my value and my endless potential.

Thank God those words lost their power over me. How wonderful that I now understood the damaging story little Linda heard and believed for so long, was not the truth. No, not any longer!

I now strive to live my life forward. Yes, looking backwards helped me understand. But the old habit of reaction and negative thoughts are now replaced with a new dimension of action and gratitude of "what is", how much I have, and how much I am. My gratitude list is long! Every day I wake up and review it. My first gratitude is that I woke up! It is not about what happened to me, what I heard and believed and made a huge, inaccurate story about. Rather, it is about how I now choose to respond and certainly not make a story out of someone else's statement or comment.

Life will always be filled with challenges and negative words. The old story and even new stories will abound, if I let them.  Alas, it is best to accept what really is, let the rest go, decide to be content and happy and know in my heart and mind that I am certainly "much more than good enough" anyway. I have value. And it comes from me! I believe in myself, a woman, a mother, an oma, a Registered Nurse, a dancer, an animal lover, and most of all, a kind and empathetic human being.

I don't have to be better than my mother or anyone else for that matter. I just have to be better than I ever thought I could have been. And I am!

Yes, I am Linda!


Linda Harrison

# Be Still

I appreciate everyone's efforts from of all walks of life who wrote a chapter in this book to share advice with others who may need inspiration in times of life's struggles. I hope that my chapter will help others as well. Since we are all unique with different life experiences, we see life and its struggles from different perspectives. Yet with all of our differences, the one common element is life itself. Today in our world with the Covid-19 virus, each one of us is encountering something no one would have imagined just months ago. The threat to life, whether to our physical lives or threat to our way of life with its liberties.

So at this time, a call to share what strengthens us or encourages us to carry on is wonderful. I must say that the most essential sources of strength and encouragement for me are faith in God and the blessings of family and true friends. While I was growing up, going to church was an important piece of my development. During my youth we had what was called "Blue Laws" that required non-essential businesses to remain closed on Sundays. It was a day that allowed us to go to church and spend the rest of the day with family without the distractions of businesses open and electronic devices to take us away from interacting with each other. It gave us time to bond closer to each other, encourage each other with love and discussions, and to have fun together. It was also a day to focus on the blessings of family and our appreciation for God.

I understood that we lived in a world created by God and that we are ultimately answerable to Him. Certainly faith in God would be a key factor in our walk through life. However, it wasn't until my adult life, after being married with two children, that my faith truly grew. With the day to day struggles of raising a family, working, and all that goes with it, having faith in God helped.

As I looked closer at the Bible for answers to just who God is, I've learned that it wasn't me, but it was He who had given me strength to get through life's struggles. There is one specific scripture which has sustained me through some of the most difficult times in my life. The verse is so simple that it could be easily overlooked, but it is my peace and tranquility in a tumultuous storm. In Psalms 46:10, the first portion says "Be still, and know that I am God."

In these times of uncertainty when our world is turning completely upside down and news headlines bring fear and anxiety, people have many more questions than answers. When I have those questions and fear, I remember that small voice in my ear that says "Be still." I remember to stop the running in circles, stop grasping for all the answers and stop my thoughts of despair. Basically STOP! BE STILL! Know that God is in control, a God who loves His creation, and allows all of us to have a relationship with Him, a relationship that brings us into God's spiritual kingdom. This spiritual kingdom is very real, perhaps more so than the physical one we are all living in now. The physical one is in upheaval now. People are trying to make sense of it. What will happen? How much will the world change?

The spiritual kingdom of which we enter into by faith is one of consistency. This kingdom is built on peace, love and joy in the Spirit of God. A faith in God gives us peace. It is a peace which surpasses all understanding. It gives me peace of heart and mind just by knowing who is ultimately in control of things.

This Covid-19 virus and other devastating events that happen in our lives, show us how little we really are in control. Realizing that no matter how smart the human race is, we are not total masters of our fate and that brings about fear. Today, we are in fear of one another so we use isolation practices, masks, gloves and little contact with others due to this fear. My recommendation for others to combat this fear is to "Stop!" Be still and focus on the One who is in control. Pray that God will provide you with a peace of heart, mind and soul which will surpass understanding and calm your fears.

Besides a faith in God, time of staying at home with family allows us to remember what's truly important in life to maintain peace and an inner desire for love and comfort. It's also a time to reflect on what blessings we possess. We have our family and friends and we have our faith in God to get us through life's trials. We should dwell on these blessings.

Steven Schilling

# Our Inner Voice

One of the best things I learned in life that has left the biggest impression in my heart, mind, body and soul is to" listen to that small, silent voice inside us".

That voice can be like a little spiritual nudge, trying to tell you something. You feel it sometimes when you wake up and someone is on your mind, or when you're going about your day and all of a sudden, out of nowhere, someone's name pops up in your mind. Or you can be at the grocery store and run into someone or you're listening to a song and you're reminded of someone else, seemingly out of the blue. I have had these spiritual nudges all throughout my life, but it has taken me many years to really pay attention to them.

It can be in a dream or even in an awake state. But however you "hear" this voice, look up, take notice and take action because God is trying to tell you something. Intuition is a beautiful gift from God. "In-tu-it".... get "into" the habit of being aware of what God is trying to tell you. If it's a person who enters your thoughts, reach out and contact them. They may need you or someone at that very moment, and it just might as well be, and can be, you.

Countless times I have forwarded an email, made a call or sent a text with a poem, just to say hi or a video or Ted Talk on something that is meaningful, and I hear from the person just how much it meant to them, as they were really down or going through something very personal and my voice lifted their spirits.

Here is my story that I hope when you hear it, will make you stop, take notice and make that call: I am a CRNA (Certified Nurse Anesthetist) and was mentored by a magnificent colleague and CRNA friend named Peter Quail. He not only was great at being a CRNA, but he could cook and bake the best baka-la, cod with Ritz crackers, and key lime pie. He could also teach difficult subjects, like neurolinguistics, and make it sound like a symphony. He could also speak Portuguese and communicate like a diplomat. I appreciated and learned so much from him. He even found me a friend in his very own daughter Amy. He was a kind, humble and gentle spirit of a man. He was one of the very reasons I became a CRNA.

Fast forward 8 years. While at work one day in the ICU, which isn't an atypical place to be outside the operating room for a CRNA, I headed toward a patient's room to prepare for a beside procedure, and heard my name being called out. What was unusual and unexpected was that it was Peter calling me from inside the ICU room.  He was in there caring for his neighbor, who had fallen ill. We got so excited to see each other. We had not seen each other since my wedding and graduation from anesthesia school eight years prior. We reminisced and promised to call each other and get together, but time went by with no contact. One year later, I awoke with Peter on my mind. So I called him. No answer. Next day, I called again. Still no answer. The next week I grew frantic trying to reach him but again to no avail. I even tried contacting him through other people we both knew, again, all to no avail. So I gave up and stopped calling him.

I don't know how long it was before I heard that silent voice inside my head and that spiritual nudge to contact him again, but when I did, I had heard that he recently passed away. He was stuck in another country while on vacation and fell ill. Because of the gravity of his illness, he passed away surrounded by his loved ones, yet many miles from home. I really believe that when you get that certain nudge to call, hug, write or visit someone, I have learned to listen to that small silent voice. It may very well be the last time you see or speak to someone. Moreover, it may be the best time to tell someone how much they mean to you, or how much you appreciate and love them. God moves us in the right direction to lift another person up when he silently speaks to us, but we need to stop and listen. Don't deny that certain spirit and voice God has put inside us all. Your attention to it could make all the difference in the world.

In loving memory of my friend and mentor - Peter Quail.

Lisa Conti

# Looking Through Rose Colored Glasses

I grew up in a small country town about one hour south of Kansas City. I was one of ten children from my dad, four of which we share the same biological mom. I was raised with my three sisters, mainly by mom. My dad had many families. Mine was his fourth. Other than my three biological sisters, I only know of two older half -brothers. When I was twelve years old, my dad left us to start his fifth family. Even when he was with my family, I only saw him on weekends as he worked in St Louis.

Our home had only four rooms. Two were bedrooms. All four sisters slept in one bedroom, two sisters to two full beds. Our house had no running water or a bathroom. We used an outhouse that we playfully called "the pink palace". We had no air conditioning. We used a box fan in a window to keep us cool on hot summer nights. We had an oil stove to heat up the living room and keep us warm in the winter. We would carry water in buckets into the house from the outside well to wash dishes and bath ourselves. We would heat the water in big pots on the stove to have hot water.

One morning, shortly after dad left us, we woke up to find he had stolen the family car. We were all devastated, especially mom, because now, aside from not having any income from dad, we were now prisoners of the rural town we lived in. But with all this happening, mom never lost her composure or focus. Somehow, she was able to work her magic and figure things out. She was able to borrow some money from a few "earth angels" and went back to work. To say my mom was an amazing woman would be a gross understatement. I don't know how she did it, where she got her strength from, but one thing I do know is that her attitude never was in doubt. She had a way of making all four daughters feel special, safe, and secure, even in the most dire of circumstances.

Two of my sisters and myself, worked throughout high school as waitresses in a small café. The couple who owned it provided these jobs to us out of kindness. They gave us a chance, an opportunity. I was thirteen years old when I started working there. I made .65 cents per hour plus any tips I would receive. This money bought my school lunches, my school books, and the fabric I needed to make my own clothes.

The fun times I experienced as a young girl centered around the eighty acres that surrounded our home. Me and my sisters used to roam the property, explore the woods, swing on grape vines for hours at a time, swim in the pond, and skip on the many rocks. We made a treehouse, really just a seat on a tree branch that we would climb up to and could see for miles everything that was around us. We would also climb the ladder to the top of our barn and jump out into a pile of hay. These were the fun times of my early childhood.

The other outlet I had was athletics. In high school, I lettered in basketball and volleyball, and ran track and played softball. My mom never missed any of mine, or my sisters' games. She was always there. She was also the chaperone to the many sock hops and other school events. She never let us down. She could, and did, do it all. At seventeen years old, I got pregnant. I just could not find the words to tell mom, but I knew she knew. And she was heartbroken. I wound up marrying the father of my baby shortly after I became pregnant. With the birth of my son, mom's heart mended, and she became an even better grandma than she was a mom. Even with my new family, my mom was always a positive influence in my life and I spent the rest of her life trying to be the best daughter I could.

In spite of my dysfunctional family and our difficult living conditions, nothing ever seemed to bother me. At the time, I didn't know that my life was a hardship. I had no idea we were poor. I just didn't know any better. And somehow, always led by mom, we all seemed to laugh almost every night. I was extremely shy, except around my family and very close friends, yet, I was the family entertainer and goofball. My one sister had a chemical imbalance, not diagnosed until many years later. She was the pit bull of the family. I learned very early on to stay away from her. She was meaner than mean. I think the reason we always clashed was that my attitude was always cheery.  She would always scold me…"take off your rose colored glasses". At the time, I had no clue what that meant.

My dad died years later, penniless.  I paid for his funeral, and was proud to do so.

My mom died in 2009. As I said earlier she was the beacon of light in my life.  Not only did she have a kind heart, common sense and a loving soul, she never seemed to let her circumstances or her surroundings effect who she was as a person, or let it influence the parenting of her daughters. It took me years to finally figure out that it was her attitude that was by far her best quality and allowed her to enjoy her life and her family, in spite of her many challenges. She was God's blessing to me. I miss her dearly. There is not a day that goes by where she does not have an influence in how I live my life.

Today, I live in a very upscale community in Bonita Springs, Florida. I am a proud daughter, a sister, a mom, a grandma, aunt, and have many friends, many of who are my childhood friends from that small town outside Kansas City. I have had several careers, including my own business.

I have always worked hard. I knew I never wanted to live the life I was born into. I have been fortunate enough to have traveled to amazing places. I have had, and continue to have an amazing life.

My memories of my mom and dad, as well as my childhood are plentiful. My dad, although not a very good man, did give me a very special gift, the gift of gab. I have used this gift throughout my life to not only serve myself, but more importantly, to serve others. And from my mom, the gifts I received are countless. She taught me that a good heart and soul were the foundation of anything else I would learn to possess. She showed me how to love and respect others. She showed me what my dreams could become if I only dared, and she the taught me the rewards of hard work. She emulated the person I knew I wanted to become. But the biggest gift she gave me was the power of a positive attitude.

As I said earlier, I have lived an amazing life, even the first seventeen years. What I've learned is this. That regardless of the hand that is dealt to you, you have the ability and the power to change anything you want. Don't wait around for others to do this for you, admit your mistakes, learn from them, keep the faith, stay focused, treat others as you would want them to treat you, be humble, work hard, and most of all, have a good attitude.

Maybe my bi polar sister was right all along. I do see the world through rose colored glasses!


Carolyn Dechman Orr

# The Invisible Front Line

Eight years ago my wife was diagnosed with Stage 4 Ovarian Cancer. Anyone who knows someone who is fighting cancer will tell you it is not just one person fighting this horrible disease, but their family and friends alike. We are all on this journey and we are all fighting the same cause. Through the years since my wife Joan's first diagnosis, she had a node removed between her lungs and had to live with and endure the pain and uncomfortableness of a Pleura Catheter for several months. I was the one who became her Caregiver and nurse. I learned how to clean and drain this Catheter and document her vittles until the catheter was removed.

After the catheter was removed, she was scheduled for surgery, which included the removal of her ovaries, appendix, gall bladder and a section of her diaphragm. We were told she would need blood, so I donated mine, and that we would be going home with Enoxaparin sodium, aka Lovenox needles. I had to have the nurses teach me how to administer the shots.

Over the past few years, my role as "Caregiver" has grown. My wife and I from day one never shared a fifty/fifty relationship. I've learned that if you're not ready to commit to a 100% relationship, then don't waste your time. A great man once said," You know you're in love when you can't fall asleep because reality is finally better than your dreams". Caring for Joan is my not my job... it's my passion. I think the true definition of "Caregiver" is Nurse, Nutritionist, Speech Therapist, Mental Health Doctor, Health Advocate, Health Care Proxy, Support Team and Friend.

During the Pandemic of 2020, Joan remained indoors because of her compromised immune system, while I limited my time outside including shopping. Washing hands while singing happy birthday twice, disinfecting a kitchen, etc. was all second nature to us. It is confusing for us to keep hearing how the rest of the world needs to be constantly reminded to wash their hands, and perform other simple tasks to help stop the spread of this virus. During this pandemic, Joan was tested for the virus a week before resuming her chemotherapy treatment with what is known as the "Brain Tickler". This procedure involves a long swab that is inserted deep into both nostrils. It is extremely uncomfortable, especially for someone who already has so many other issues. Thankfully she tested negative. Each day during this Coronavirus outbreak I needed to be sure she was safe from this COVID-Phenomena, so I checked her vitals daily and listened to her lungs for vascular congestion. We both wear masks in public as well as latex gloves.

There are those who say this Virus is a hoax. I do not allow myself the luxury of believing this because I am a Caregiver, entrusted to care for the person I love most in this world. I chose to look at it from a different perspective. Let's look at the bible for example. Some say it is made up of stories, a hoax, fake news if you will. When you die, you die. There is no heaven or hell, just end of life. Then there are those who choose to believe that if you accept God into your life, you go to heaven. I choose to believe in the latter. Let's for a moment, assume I'm right. If I am, then when I die, I go to heaven. There is a reward. But let's assume I am wrong. There is no heaven and all I did was just lead a good life with no reward. I did no harm to myself or to anyone.

The same thing applies to this virus. If there is no virus, I do no harm; no one is injured or worse. But if there is a virus, those who call it a hoax may be killing innocent people because of their choices. I choose to wear a mask and be socially conscious with the intent to keep others safe. I can't and won't take the chance that I guessed wrong, not only because I am a Caregiver, but because it may put other people at risk.

October is Breast Cancer awareness month. Everyone wears pink. September is Ovarian Cancer Awareness month and people wear Teal (we think outside the bra). Here is a little known fact. Did you know that the woman who created the pink ribbon to make us aware of breast cancer died of ovarian cancer?

Here's an idea. What if we took a two-inch long piece of teal ribbon and cut a simple "V" at one end and wore it each September, the Start of flu season, as a reminder of the pandemic of 2020 and the pandemics of the past. The pandemic of 2020 could easily be World War Three. This flat teal ribbon would be a reminder to all of us that we must stay vigilant and must not forget. For those of us who choose to ignore history, we will be destined to repeat it. September could become the month where we "Teal" the world to stay vigilant and flatten the curve. If we join together as Caregivers we can wear our flat teal ribbons to remind everyone that we never want to endure a pandemic like this ever again.


Keith Happ

# Moments

"Stretching His Hand Up To Reach For The Stars, Too Often Man Forgets The Flowers At His Feet"
-Jeremy Bentham

Amidst the chaos of a pandemic that has diabolically woven its way through every crevice of our lives, thoughts that were deeply and neatly buried in my mind have slowly come to the surface. I am waiting for my soon to be life of retirement. Saying goodbye to a life I knew for many years. A life I loved. Teaching children to read has not only been my profession, it's been my passion. I am waiting with a knot in my stomach for my new life to approach. Why the knot, you might ask? Always a knot, I will tell you, as so many of my friends would attest to. That's me, the ultimate worrier. Someone who would neatly plan out her days and her future, creating possible raging fires in my mind, then attempting to extinguish them before they would appear.

Most times, there were no fires, maybe just little puffs of smoke. Reaching out for a life that won't hurt me and doing everything in my power to stop any hurt before it appeared. I spent so much of my life living with the racing thoughts, the "what ifs", rather than living life right there in the moment. I was seeing life through a somewhat distorted lens that was blurred by my thoughts and fears, never really appreciating or focusing on what was really important. I believe many of us do unknowingly. Did we ever take that moment, reflect and assess who we are and what our impact on this world might be? If we did that, did we do things to make meaningful change to those things that needed to be addressed? Maybe in some ways some of us did, but because of the blurred lens of how I approached life, I didn't.

However, over the spring months of 2020, everything changed as a result of two terrible viruses that swept through our world. All those racing thoughts I had, like a proverbial hamster on the wheel, were forced to come to a screeching halt the day the first deadly virus, the coronavirus, or COVID-19, reached out its tentacles to basically anyone it could get hold of and wrap itself around. Life as we knew it stopped. The sprints from work to the gym and all the extras of living a regular life stopped. Squeezing in time with friends and family, maybe a quick mani/pedi and some hair maintenance stopped. No sports to play or watch, no restaurants were opened to be on time for. Broadway went dark. No more racing around of body or mind.

As an educator, I was always concerned when parents would confess that school work would be put aside because of so many extra-curricular activities. Soccer practice or dance classes or baseball, children just so overbooked. Everyone was running in so many directions every day. Our society, as we knew it, seemed so concerned with moving up the ladder of how many "things" one could acquire, accumulating trophies we can show off to our neighbors along the way. We did it with material things, we did it with the hope of pushing our kids to achieve greatness. As I look back on my life, I too wanted it all, driving nice cars, remodeling my house, even working at an expensive sleep-away camp so my children could have the "best" experience. Having goals are always good, but I always felt we were losing something so important along the way. My gut often whispered "something's very off". Would I do things differently now, looking back? I know I would.

So when the "monster" we called coronavirus blanketed the world, life, the runaway train as we knew it, stopped dead in its tracks and my mind stopped running. While the virus brought so much tragedy and fear, the likes we've never known, it also single handedly removed our "normal" concerns in one swift knockout punch. What it left in its wake were families bonding together at home and communicating with each other and children spending more time with their families than ever before.  To me, that was a good thing. Families stopped running. We were forced into a spiritual hibernation, and with that, something slowly emerged. Our souls awakened. We actually looked around and took in the moment. We opened our eyes and "saw" the people and things that really mattered to us, probably for the first time in a very long time. We all took a collective cleansing breath. We started noticing each other, rather than things. We were forced to stay in the moment, something that myself and fellow worriers always struggled to do. As new and radical as that thinking of "staying in the moment" has always been for me, I must admit, I felt like the weight of continual worry had finally lifted. I had been forced to be in the moment and I was actually savoring every single one of them now.

As I write this, the TV is on in the background. I look up and watch the first launching of astronauts from U.S. soil in nine years has just lifted off, soaring into the sky towards the International Space Station. Just like we do, the spaceship reaches for the stars. What a wonderful moment the launch has brought to our country - a new, exciting beginning. Almost simultaneously, however, another virus reared its ugly head. Riots were breaking out all over the world because a man of color, George Floyd, was murdered by a police officer. Police brutality of black and brown people has been a common theme in this country, spreading its own kind of deadly virus throughout the years. Too often, the cries of the people shouting "Black Lives Matter" was ignored. Life as we knew it changed the day George Floyd took his last breath. That man was killed by the virus of racism and apathy. We as a society, had to stop in our tracks once again as we gazed in horror at Mr. Floyd's lifeless body under the foot of a police officer. Just as the coronavirus did, our eyes once again were forced wide open.  With raw emotion, a revolution was born. Cries of protest were heard all over the world. There's now a strong possibility that the chant "Black Lives Matter" will change from chant to reality.

The viruses have taken so much away, but they've also given us something very special in return. They made us stop and think. We are more in the moment than ever before and this time, hopefully, we have a clear lens guiding us. Maybe the really important things in life will no longer be overlooked and ignored.  As we look at life with this fresh new lens, we might want to redirect our thinking about things that really matter, rather than worrying needlessly about things that don't. That is my promise to myself. I hope with all my heart it will be a promise others make as well.

So when we all set out to reach for the stars, maybe this time we won't forget to stop and look at the flowers at our feet.


Ellen Ballaban

# Life Is Not A Dress Rehearsal

This title really explains how I see each day. I try not to worry about the things I have no control over , or any other things that may happen in life, even though at times I sometimes try to squeeze too much into each day.

My very early years were not very happy. Having two parents with a drinking problem, it left me with very little sense of family. I grew up mainly on my own with no guidance or structure. I married very young for all the wrong reasons. I thought that marriage would give me the chance to create the perfect family. I was going to be the perfect wife, mother and homemaker. But love was missing in that marriage, and it ended after ten years in divorce. The best thing that came out of that marriage was my three wonderful children. They are what I am most proud of. Divorce was difficult, both financially and emotionally. I had no family to ask for help as I was an only child, but learned from a young age that I had to make my life become what it would be. Life is not a dress rehearsal, you only get to live it once and I was not about to feel sorry for myself.

I worked my butt off to allow my family to stay in our home. I was fortunate enough to get a job in a small family owned business. The company grew, and I worked hard, and grew with it. After working for that company for 36 years, I retired as Director Of Sales & Service. I traveled all over the country as we had offices in almost every state. My career was great. Financially, I had no more worries. Life was good. I even remarried after many years alone.

I watched all my three children go through college and graduate.  My son works on Wall Street and is very successful. My one daughter graduated as a Physical Therapist and now is the Vice President of all therapies at St Charles Hospital. My other daughter is a Guidance Counselor.   All three children are married. What happened next is the most wonderful thing that has ever happened to me, they provided me with nine grandchildren. They make me smile every time I see or just think of them.

 After twenty five years of marriage to my second husband, he informed me that he was no longer happy and I experienced my second divorce The home I fought so hard over the years to keep was now way too big for just me. I had never been alone my entire life. My husbands, my kids, or my sick mom was always with me. But in time, mom passed on and the kids all married. I felt so alone. But I knew it was time to start all over again. I was the loneliest and saddest I had ever been in my life, just completely lost. What do I do at fifty plus years old?

 What I have learned is this... life is never easy. You have to roll with the punches. You cannot just sit back and let life pass you by. You do not get another shot at it. This is it. Life is not a dress rehearsal.

One day, a small add in the local paper changed my life. This is what it said : "Arthur Murray, $80... learn how to dance. ".  Well that led to meeting so many wonderful people in the dance world who became my closest friends.  Besides, I loved learning how to dance.  I would go to the dance socials alone...so frightened to go in. Afterwards, driving home would be sad, as the house I was returning to was dark and still I was all alone. Why I asked?  I didn't want or plan for this.  But I realized that no-one is going to change my life but me.  No sense looking back, I can't change the past.  Just look forward and proceed onward. And then at one of the dance socials, I met a man whose name was Fred.  He was a gift from God. He changed everything. My life is now everything I hoped it would be.

I truly believe we have to look for the happiness in life, even though life may not always give it to us. I've always seen the good in people, not the bad. I have always been willing to try something new. Life is not a Dress Rehearsal. I truly believe that. I made mistakes along the way, and wish I did things differently sometimes, but I cannot undo the past. I can only try to make the future better. It's up to me. No one else can do that for me.

Fred and I have been together for almost 15 years. We've been married for almost 10.   He has and continues to add so much value to my life.  A chance meeting coupled with a gift of faith, started our adventure together.   Since then, I have never looked back. My life right now is like living a dream.   Every day is like being on a great vacation. I get up every morning and appreciate my good fortune. I make sure to enjoy every day, sometimes maybe even too much.  But time goes by so fast, and I want to make sure to appreciate everything while I can.

I would love everyone to feel as I do. Here is the lesson I've learned. No matter what curves life throws at you, try to enjoy every day.  See the good in people and all that's around you. Remove the negatively in your life.  Life is not a Dress Rehearsal. It works for me.

Chris Martin

# Know Thyself

Early on in my life's journey, I envisioned a stable and productive life filled with happiness, family ties, children, grandchildren, and enjoying our time together. An abundance of photos layered in boxes justified and captured it all. Each and every photo was from a moment in time that had portrayed me in various moods of happiness.

When I accepted the challenge of writing a chapter in this book, it allowed me to share the highlights of what I have learned to value in life. The exercise seemed like it was going to be a cakewalk. But to my surprise, it wasn't. I have always been true to myself and have learned to trust my own instincts. I have always believed in a quote from the ancient philosopher, Aristotle," Know thyself".

I have found that at your deepest inner self, it's important to know who you are, what your goals are, what your dreams are, and what your convictions are. It's also important to know your self-worth, because this is your essence, your life's sense of purpose and meaning. Your heart has packaged all this away for you, including the will to survive life's curveballs.  This is what enables you to pull yourself up through adversity. It gives you the tools to survive injustices and fear of the unknown, because you know who you are and what you can handle.

This current pandemic has given me that insight. It made me realize the future isn't as important as the present, that focusing on family and myself would now become an important part of my daily life. I was reminded to savor the moments of peace, and the sanctuary of my own home, to finish reading a book, to find a new recipe, to learn a new skill, to face time old friends, to clean closets, to keep a diary, and to allow my grandchildren to have a keepsake when I am no longer here, so they could better know who I was. Time during this crisis seems to have stopped still, but this time is our opportunity to take advantage and recognize not what is to come, but what we can do today.

Life holds many scenarios, challenges, accomplishments, as well as sadness's. Friends will come and go, even the ones we depend on to be there forever, even a spouse I took vows with and expected to be there until the end of time. These are the challenges that life can give us. How we handle them depends on how much we know ourselves and how much we trust ourselves. We should never choose to allow someone to alter our behavior, undermine our genuineness, or change who we are. Otherwise our purpose and vision of our path become a meaningless stretch of time that hinders us from moving mentally forward. We cannot be true to ourselves, make choices, forgive, embrace or have hope for our future, if we don't look inside ourselves and learn who we are.

Time has a way of easing the pain of hardships and mistakes. If it wasn't for a keen awareness of who I was, I could not imagine what I could overcome today. Losing my husband to a serious illness in 2005, the downturn of the real estate market, a business magazine entity owned by my husband, all turned into one nightmare after another. While some family and friends would give help and advice, his best friend ignored my need for help.

It made me realize I needed to live by my own force moving forward. I became focused on keeping the business going until I could sell it.  And I did. But not without many shed tears. It wasn't easy to simply walk away with the economy down, unemployment up, and businesses just trying to stay afloat. But with a sense of dedication to his memory and my resilience, I learned I had the power and confidence to continue.

As I look back, it gives me a great sense of accomplishment because I found that at my weakest moment, I became the strongest. If you have the will, the determination and the desire to change, you will. What I also learned is that in all our lives, even in spite of all the mistakes and hardships, it is all just temporary, a moment in time. Knowing myself has guided me through the roughest of times and gives full meaning to the best of times. Know yourself. With your deepest inner self you will find your own path and trust yourself through your life's journey where your capabilities lie.

Terri Romano

# Be A Survivor

Someone said that Life is a series of moments and moments are always changing, just like thoughts, both negative and positive. I think all of us who are of a certain age, can affirm that statement, as we have so many experiences, both negative and positive to relate to. I often think about that, especially when I'm sitting in the dentist chair, or experiencing a similar negative event. It's only a moment!

There is another thought that I firmly think about, and have incorporated as something like a motto in my life, which I discovered about myself about twenty five years ago. It was a time of tremendous stress and change occurring to me, as I was going through the breakup of my marriage. Like many people in that situation I was hurting, feeling like a failure, and in a state of overwhelming uncertainty. I had a number of sessions with a counselor to try and bring clarification and fortification for my situation.

Now as anyone can tell you, one of the benefits of counseling is introspection, where you examine or observe your own mental and emotional processes. During this process, for me the most eye-opening experience had to do with my past and how I arrived at the place where I was. Because I was in a real funk at the time, during my sessions, I kept thinking and focusing on so many of the negative aspects of my life, while glossing over the really positive ones. Then after a few sessions, I will never forget what the counselor observed about my life... and me. He said; "Fred, you are a survivor", and those simple words and what they meant to me, forever changed the way I think of my life.

So that's my advice. When things are happening, whether positive and especially negative, remember. ...You are a survivor.


Fred Martin

# We Only Have Ourselves

I would like to take this opportunity to share my experience as to why I believe self- reliance is essential in our lives and bring awareness onto why people seem to rely on others in search of their own happiness and why we seem to give away our power.

Over the years I have noticed men and women relying on others for happiness. I've noticed time and again that these people sometimes succeed, but mostly fail. They continue to set themselves up for disappointment. They keep searching for the perfect friend or partner. They seek happiness from others. Their preconceived notions turn out unfulfilled, only to hear the words "if only" when their relationship fails. These observations often lead me to think about the phrase, "We're born alone, we live alone, and we die alone." Is it really true?

I grew up in the suburbs of Long Island, New York, in a somewhat upper middle class neighborhood. I married in my late 20s and had two beautiful sons. My husband was from Sardinia, Italy. Unfortunately, he died at the age of forty-one, when I was only thirty-nine and my two sons were four and six. I did my best to raise my boys to be good, honest human beings and to respect others, especially women. We lived in a very traditional "family oriented" neighborhood. I was a single mom raising two little boys. I enrolled them in various sports activities such as swimming lessons, baseball, bowling etc. I often took them on chartered fishing boats so they could learn to fish. Since my husband was gone, I often wondered why I never really felt alone, although I probably should have; especially noticing the way some people often viewed and sometimes judged me. I guess I was too focused on raising my boys and knew I needed to find my own power. I had to encourage them to do their best and eventually find their own way in life. Not only were they very young and just beginning their life's journey, they were doing so with just one parent, all the while dealing with their own pain and loss of their dad. I remember sitting in the stands of their baseball games, watching them play, or should I say, mostly not playing.  My observation is that the coach was more apt to play the boys whose fathers were present and vocal, sad, but true. Some say it takes a village, but I found in a lot of situations, it was mostly up to me to keep them focused and valued.

I learned that if it was going to be, then it would have to be up to me. I was the main force in their lives. I became self- empowered and learned not to doubt my decisions, as I know they were always born out of love and came from my heart.  What I became sure about was never to doubt myself.

The times in my life where I let others make decisions for me were not only a mistake, but led to poor outcomes. I know now that it was my mistake for allowing others to take control, when I instinctively knew what was in my and my sons' best interest. The misjudgments I made in this regard led to dark moments that cannot be reversed.  I learned not to give them more power by dwelling on them and learned to let them go and move onward with renewed vision. I thank God for giving me the insight and power to have let go of these oversights. What I learned is this. It's ok to listen and evaluate the advice of others, but learn to trust yourself.  I learned to listen to that inner voice inside me. No one else knows what's right for me, except me.

So again, here is a question I grapple with. Are we really alone?

I have found that you can be in a relationship and still feel alone. There was a time where I entered into a relationship that I should not have been in. I compromised my values and in doing so, myself. In the beginning I was blinded to the chaos in this person and his life. He wanted to control everything, even my sons. As the years passed the relationship became so parasitic, so chaotic, and so toxic, I knew I had to get out. Finding a peaceful moment was a rarity. Thankfully, I awakened, and found the strength to get out and end the nightmare. I was never more alone than in this relationship.

So in answer to the question, are we really alone, no, we aren't, not always. However, I do believe that even in spite of the well-intended people who truly do want to help, I believe in the final analysis, we really have to rely on ourselves and find our own power and peace. If we are able to find this peace and respect within ourselves, and find the value in our own choices, I believe that these qualities, by themselves, can lead to happiness.

Orson Welles wrote:
"We're born alone, we live alone, and we die alone. Only through our love and friendship can we create the illusion for the moment we are not alone."

Another question I often ask is: Why is it that when we look at the choices we sometimes make, we all seem to battle both internal and external chaos. Do we create this chaos ourselves?

The external chaos comes from situations we either can't, or refuse to control. We somehow allow it to damage our inner calm. We need to recognize it as external, keep it there, and not let it affect our inner calm. Ships don't sink because water is all around them. They sink because water gets inside them.

The Covid 19 pandemic is now the external chaos going on all over the world. It is a virus that to this point, we cannot control. But internally we can control how we react to it. What surprises me is that many people thought something like this could never happen. We have so much power to live a beautiful life, yet as a species, we appear to be on a course to create our own destruction. Do we not see this? What are we becoming?  How is it that during this pandemic a 46- year- old man in Minneapolis is brutally held down for close to nine minutes and suffocated while others watched and allowed it to happen? Look at the chaos this created. Could all of this have been avoided?

What has happened is cause and effect, or should I say causality. The meaning (from Wikipedia) "is influence by which one event, process or state, a cause, contributes to the production of another event, process or state, an effect, where the cause is partly responsible for the effect, and the effect is partly dependent on the cause. In general, a process has many causes, which are also said to be casual factors for it, and all lie in its past. An effect can in turn be a cause of, or casual factor for many other effects, which all lie in its future.

Yes, the meaning is as complicated as the situation we are facing.

So here are the things I have learned from this pandemic and from my past life experiences. Your universal guidance comes from your inner voice. Your inner voice is a gift, receive it, and don't doubt it. Allow space for it to enter. Give yourself time to embrace life. Don't put yourself in situations you don't want to be in. Learn to say no. Don't do anything your conscious tells you not to do. My life is valuable therefor my time is precious. I have learned that my external order will promote a healthier inner peace. I have learned to embrace life even with all of its uncertainties and chaos and hope for a better tomorrow, as I live for today.

Susan E. Saiu

# My "Story"

Did you ever encounter people who seem to have very strong opinions about certain things, who are convinced that their opinion is the correct one? Do you notice how these people dig their heels in and reaffirm their opinions every time someone else has a different viewpoint? I used to be one of these people. I was convinced that my beliefs, my viewpoint, my knowledge was the correct one. As I matured, I learned that these viewpoints were not only inaccurate, and contrary to what other people may be feeling, but were nothing more than a "story" I had created inside myself.

This "story" I created did not purport the truth. It merely conveyed the truth as I knew it. And this "story" that I created, did not happen overnight. It was developing and formalizing inside me ever since birth. My upbringing, my education, my belief systems, in fact every experience I've ever had all had a role in creating my "story". When I opened my eyes and finally took notice of this, I realized that my "story" was only right to me.

People listening to me, even if they did not recognize that I was merely repeating my "story" as I understood it, either agreed or disagreed with it. If they shared my beliefs and agreed with me, I had an ally. But if they disagreed, I found myself defending my "story" until I could convince them of its merit. What I didn't realize at the time was that in trying to convince these non-believers of my "story", they were not only reciting their "stories" to me, but trying to convince me of theirs as well. Not only was I not convincing them to the merits of my "story", and they me, I found myself judging their stories to the standards of my own story.

Each of us only knows what we know. We also know what we don't know. But it's that which we don't know, that we don't know, that becomes the most important factor. We can only repeat what we know and believe, and as such, make a determination of what is right and what is wrong. Some of the stories we aspire to, were created by our parents, our teachers and our friends. I learned from my parents what they learned from their parents, even my teachers could only teach me what they knew. These "stories" that we learned exist solely within our own head. The more we repeat them, the more powerful and entrenched we become in them and we create an internal power that convinces us that our "story" is the correct one. Our "stories" are also constantly in a state of flux. They are guided by how we may be feeling at the time, both emotionally and physically. Such factors as jealousy, anger, loneliness, fear, frustration, as well as joy and happiness all play a factor in how our "stories" are communicated. They become our reality, but we are projecting a false reality because our "story" is only true for us in our current state of mind.

When I began to understand that other people's "stories" were not necessarily wrong because they differed from mine, I no longer felt the need to be right. I became more accepting of other's viewpoints and found that when I changed the way I viewed my 'story", my world opened up and life became more enjoyable. I no longer saw the world through my eyes only.  And I recognize that someone else's "story", as well as my story, may not be the real truth. There are no versions of the actual truth. The truth is the truth whether we or anybody else accepts it.

I've learned that when I listen and acknowledge other people's "stories" and stopped trying to convince them of mine, like magic, my world changed. I found myself to be more accepting of others and more importantly, they of me. No longer did I feel the need to defend myself or to convince others. While doing this, my life for the most part did not change. But what did change, is the interaction I had with others. Simply put, I changed myself and everything around me changed. People became less combative and I became happier.

Dr. Wayne Dyer so eloquently says: "Judgement means that you view the world as you are, not as it is".

When we tell or listen to any "story", we create emotions. These emotions are real, we don't fake them. The trick, as I have learned, is to become more aware of the impact these emotions have over our "stories", and even though we all have lapses, I believe your relationships and hence your life will improve. But this is a choice. When I learned not to retreat into the familiar actions of the past, and looked for a new, different and more intuitive path, I found that more and more people wanted to actually listen to my "story". And I found that opening my mind to other people's "stories" actually opens the door to greater knowledge, because I was better able to understand the other side of an issue, and became more conversant in my own expanded and revised "story'.

Take it from me, not feeling the need to project your "story", and listening to other peoples "stories" can cause you to be happier than you ever thought possible.


Tom Fallarino

Made in the USA
Middletown, DE
20 July 2020